More Altars of REMEMBRANCE

God's indescribable love and protection

HANNAH HOFER

WESTBOW
PRESS®
A DIVISION OF THOMAS NELSON
& ZONDERVAN

WestBow Press books may be ordered through booksellers or by contacting:

WestBow Press
A Division of Thomas Nelson & Zondervan
1663 Liberty Drive
Bloomington, IN 47403
www.westbowpress.com
844-714-3454

Scripture taken from the New King James Version® Copyright © 1982 by Thomas Nelson. Used by permission. All rights reserved.

ISBN: 978-1-6642-1793-5 (sc)
ISBN: 978-1-6642-1794-2 (e)

Print information available on the last page.

WestBow Press rev. date: 02/25/2021

Beloved,

sharing with you the unbelievable joy God brought into my life after saving my four children and me in 1974, it brings back to mind His loving and patient work in our lives. Not learning English till I came to America at the age of 21, as a new wife and mother, I had to make my citizenship. Even though I was homesick and missed my big loving family, I was determined to make America my second home in spite of opposition.

Never would I have imagined the adventure it would be after God saved me at the age of thirty seven and how He turned even the hard and painful times into experiencing joy and knowing Him better. This is when He began to build my trust in Him. My Lord never gets tired of assuring me of His deep and never-ending love and His serious protection over those who trust Him.

After God had taken over my heart and soul, He reminded me of some special times of His protection during the war in Germany. One of my new Christian friends shared with me that this was because my Lord knew that some day in the future we would all four give our lives to Him. Because of this our children and all who followed entered His kingdom as well.

In my first book "Altars of Remembrance", by Hannah Hofer, I shared about falling in love, getting married, having our first baby Carmelita, (we call her Lita) and when she was six month old, coming to America. The next fourteen years were very happy ones, getting our first home and adding three more children, Christina, Stephen and William.

When my mother-in-law started talking at the table, I did not know if she was talking about me. So I went to the library, got myself a book and tape and spoke English in no time. It was not hard for me to get used to my new life in the U.S. and liking it.

However, I was homesick and missed my mom and two sisters as well as the rest of my very large family.

Only God had no room in our hearts and lives even though we had been told that He existed. My husband was discharged from the Army after his three- year term and became a Policeman in our city, and he loved it. All of our family were proud of him and supported him strongly in this venture.

I was proud of my husband's job and enjoyed being active in the Police-wife-club. Sadly, in the 15th year of our marriage things changed and Bill was hardly home anymore. I was hopeless because I did not know what to do and had no one I wanted to confide in. One day he walked up to me and said he wanted a divorce and walked out the door.

Billy, our six -month old son, had been watching his 2 ½ year old brother Stephen, playing ball with me in the kitchen. When Stephen noticed that his dad had not fully closed the door when he left, he quickly went out the door, starting to run after his father, wanting a ride.

When Bill, my husband, brought Stephen back inside, I was still frozen from the news, leaning against the sink. As he pushed his boy back in the house he said ruffly "take care of him" and he closed the door securely this time.

Continuing life without my husband was a very painful and lonely time and it scared me to raise our four children alone. Hoping to find a nice man to help me raise my kids, I began to go out dancing with other divorced ladies I met at my daughter's school. It did not take me long to realize that the men I met at these places had just left their own families and were not about to take on a woman with four children.

The following three years were full of hurt and a longing to be loved. One night I was laying on my living room floor crying out all the hurt of the past three years. I yelled out that if God really existed as I had been told, now would be a good time to help me. Never imagining that He heard me or even cared, I fell asleep.

So, on a very hot day in July I picked up my makeup bag and walked to my assigned territory where I was supposed to sell makeup. I could not have imagined that this would be the most important day of my life, otherwise my spirit would not have been so discouraged and depressed.

CONTENTS

The Lord's plan of Salvation 1

A wonderful new job 3

Life in our beautiful mountains 5

Additional ways for me to minister overseas 9

Poland, the other part of my DNA 13

Still More ministry 16

More about Camp Pendleton ministry 18

Another trip to Kentucky 21

Continuing growth 25

The power of prayer 27

Search for Me and you will find Me 29

Walking in His way and growing 31

The wonder and life changing way of forgiveness 33

Truly a new creation? 35

One of the awesome Christian gatherings 36

So many answered prayers 38

His protection is awesome and constant 40

Another Kentucky and Colorado visit 42

The most painful adventure of my life 45

The Four Spiritual Laws 54

THE LORD'S PLAN OF SALVATION

At the first door a young woman named Donna asked me in and offered me a glass of iced water, inviting me to sit down. I told her that I was on foot, because my oldest child had taken my car, took it for a joyride with her friends and totaled it. Donna asked if I would like to give this all to the Lord, but I had no idea what she was talking about.

She pulled out a little yellow booklet that said: "Have you heard of the Four Spiritual Laws?", asking if she could read it to me. She had been so kind to me, so I agreed. Not knowing what this was all about, I felt strangely drawn to this event not wanting to pull away from it.

The booklet said that God loves me and has a wonderful plan for my life and explained why we need a Savior. It told that if we invite Him into our heart and life, He would forgive us for everything we have done wrong so we can live with Him forever. Since I was desperate and was planning suicide, I needed to see if He was telling the truth.

So, I said that prayer and noticed that my heart was not quite so discouraged the rest of the day. I was anxious to read the Bible

Donna had given me, it was the first one I ever had. Strangely I desired to give God a try and for some reason, what I learned made sense and I longed to find out more about Him.

God said in His Bible that He truly loves me, and I realized that I was beginning to love Him too. This caused me to spend more time in His Word and I could not stop spending time with Him. Getting my kids ready for school took no time because I was anxious to get back to finding out about God loving me.

My two sons learned early about this awesome God by our daily Bible studies and the really good church our friend Donna had led us to. We loved attending Community Bible Church and were there as often as possible, especially for our beloved AWANA club which taught us to memorize Scriptures, of which.

Also my two daughters gave their lives to the Lord as did their boyfriends who later on became their husbands. This God could save them from eternal destruction and if they believed in Him. He said He would give them never ending life with Him, in a place He says, is more beautiful than they can imagine.

A WONDERFUL NEW JOB

Since my ex-husband Bill had died after a series of strokes, there was no more income for the children and me. This meant I had to find a job for our income. I tried everywhere without any success and after three weeks I was discouraged. Coming home one day, I dropped in a chair and said Jesus would you help me please?

Suddenly the phone rang and a manly voice said "this is Campus Crusade for Christ, are you still looking for a job? Stunned I said "yes". The voice continued "full time?" I answered "yes". The voice said "can you start on Monday? (this was Thursday) I said "yes". The manly voice instructed "report to the Accounting department at 8pm please."

Totally overwhelmed I said to the Lord "accounting? but Father, I'm a doctor's assistant, besides You know I never liked math". Well, I reported Monday morning and was greeted by a very nice gentleman named Barney, who kindly and patiently taught me account receivable. After the first five days I told the Lord each day that I would have to quit because it was too hard for me, then it began to make sense.

So, now I have been 43 years with this awesome Evangelical Ministry of Campus Crusade For Christ, 38 years of it have been with the Jesus Film Project. To this day I am still loving every minute of it, these were years of learning, how to evangelize and lead the lost into waiting arms of Jesus Christ the Savior.

NOW!!! I shared the above for those who have not read my first book called "Altars Of Remembrance" by Hannah Hofer". Not using my married name or a picture of me was very important to me because I feared pride entering my heart, which usually comes before the fall.

Also it made sense to me using the New King James Version for the Scriptures in my books because that is the version I use in teaching the more than 450 youths a month by Bible studies. It is the version we use in "The Juvenile Hall Detention Center" and also at "The Joy Company' a ministry to schools" which I am a part of.

The title of the book was taken from Deuteronomy27:6. Whenever God did something great for the Israelites, like at the parting of the Jordan river, He told them to build an altar of twelve large stones, one stone for every tribe of Israel. These stones were to remember the miracle God had performed there. It was also for their children, when they asked what this altar was for, they could tell them of God's faithfulness.

When I asked the Lord what to call His book, since it was His book, He impressed on me strongly "Altars of Remembrance". It is important to me that this second book would make sense to the readers, so the above is a very short version of the first book and is missing all the beautiful miracles this God of love did in our lives.

LIFE IN OUR BEAUTIFUL MOUNTAINS

H aving a friend who knew of my love for the mountains, he and his wife bought my house in the valley which I had for sale because my two sons and I longed to live in the mountains. This brought about the next miracle in our lives. Asking the Lord to do once again His perfect will and only what He wanted for us, I signed, being totally at peace, the papers for the sale.

My two daughters were married now, so it was the boys and I and we were anxious to find out what God's next plan was. For the part of the money that was mine from the sale of our home, my friend let us live in the lovely house he and his wife owned next door to them, and we could live there for five years rent free.

The house was located in the mountain city of Crestline which is 4,613' feet high and of course has lots of snow in the winter. I really liked the daily rides up and down to work, which was at the beautiful Arrowhead Springs Hotel in the San Bernardino mountains. Using my favorite melodies, I made up words of praise to my God to them and my ride would be over in no time.

Once again it was the perfect plan of our beloved God because in five years my boys would be in the service and I would be moving back to the valley. Both my sons attended Rim High School and the bus system transported them to and from school and they loved it. Bill was also a volunteer fireman on the weekends in our city of Crestline. He really enjoyed that and I was told that he was good at it.

About a ten minute walk from the school was a big "Lutheran Camp" and both my guys were offered a jobs in their kitchen. Excitedly they told me about it when they came home that day, mentioning that they could help a little with the utility bills and their clothes. When I picked them up at 9 pm after they had finished at the camp, I realized how long and dark and very curvy the ride home was.

Of course it would be much worse once the snow was on the ground. Driving already up and down daily to my job, the pick-up would have been too much for me. Sadly, I began to explain to my boys that they would not be able to keep that job, when they told me that God, as usual, had already taken care of that situation.

With great joy they explained that the head cook at the camp was a lady in our church. She said for them to tell me that she would be glad to bring them home the five days of each week since she only lived seven minutes away from us. Not only did she deliver them safely every school day, but she sent home some of the leftovers from the daily meals.

We thanked our Lord with grateful hearts. In no way could we have prayed for what our precious God arranged, only His awesome imagination could come up with this. This continued until both had graduated from high school and first Steve and then Bill had joined the service.

Steve has always been an artist and loved to draw cartoons and continued through high school. however in his last year he joined the Army but he kept up his talent there. Steve received several awards for his creative designs on Army equipment, especially trucks and on a company logo.

While they were growing up I told my boys that two jobs that would always be needed. That would be policemen and firemen and I asked God to give them wisdom in this. Well, that is the direction they both took. Stephen for 17 years as a Policeman in our city and Bill is still a volunteer Fireman for his city in Kentucky.

Not until both boys had joined the service did I need to leave the city of Crestline. It was too hard for me to live up there alone in spite of my love for the mountains. My daughters had married and were living with their families in the valley. My job was there also, as well as the three ministries I was involved in by now.

A dear friend asked me to come and live with her till I could find something permanent. The Lord continued with more guidance and growth in my life, even though I had a hard time with the empty nest experience. However, God worked it out for me to enter a personal ministry at the city's Juvenile Hall Detention Center to represent Campus Crusade for Christ.

My four children were grown now and lived with their families, but we always stayed in touch. If there is no birthday or a holiday to have a party for, we will make one up. It was awesome to me that I had eight grandchildren and fourteen great grandchildren by then and it was a joy to teach them about the God that loved them so much.

I wanted to be absolutely sure that when Jesus comes to take His children home, I would not have to worry that they were left behind. My daily prayers for them and their families are to this day that He would guide and direct them and they would never to leave His side. For this prayer I used one of God's precious scripture:

Isaiah 55:10 which says that as the rain and snow come down from heaven and do not return without watering the earth and make it sprout, so is His word that goes out from His mouth: it will not return to Him empty without accomplishing what He desires and achieving the purpose for which He sent it.

And He has kept this promise and will do so as long as I pray daily for them and every new one coming into this family, even the in-laws. As soon as I find out that one of my grandchildren and now the great grands have a boyfriend or girlfriend I found out the name and added them to my prayer list.

This faithful God also continues to have me involved and busy in ministry which keeps me from being lonely and getting into trouble. My daily times in His blessed word keeps leading me to share with others His wisdom and loving guidance written in His letter to them. By this precious time in God's continuous advice and revelations, I began to recognize His beloved voice.

ADDITIONAL WAYS FOR ME TO MINISTER OVERSEAS

O nce my children were gone from home, Campus Crusade for Christ, now called CRU, began to send me on mission trips and it opened a whole new vision for my prayers. There are too many to share them all, so I shared a few in my first book and now I will tell of another one. This trip was to India, we showed the Jesus Film almost every night.

The results were such a blessing because the viewers responded in large numbers. Most of them were willing to come to follow up Bible classes to learn more about his Savior called Jesus. We started in Deli going to the other end of the country as far as Bangalor. The showings were set up by people who had received Jesus as Lord and Savior in previous presentations.

Now they wanted their fellow country men and women to get to know Him also. Many times the only place that has electricity was the village temple and the Lord influenced the village elders to plug our generator in there. Often the screen goes up right in front of their major Idol and some other idols surround the screen which is showing our Jesus Film.

On one next showing it was planned for me to interview a pastor, I will call him Joseph. He was saved, trained and then ordained by Campus Crusade. Besides starting his own church, using our Jesus Film, he began eight more churches which were growing in membership. However, he had a most unusual beginning as he was starting his own facility.

There were marauding bands which came to raid and ravage on a regular basis in that part of the land. One of them came again with about 100 men riding into the church property. The pastor had been told the previous time that he was never to teach about this man called Jesus again. However, it was impossible for pastor Joseph to stop praising and glorifying the Savior Jesus.

The pastor was badly beaten while his pregnant wife was forced to stand next to him and watch. She was in prayer through it all. The brave man of God asked if, before they kill him, he could have just ten minutes to speak. They allowed him to speak.

He told me that he gave the best testimony of Jesus he had ever given and the result was unbelievable. The leader of this band, I will call him Ben, never got of his horse but commanded his men to turn and leave, which was exactly what they did.

It was less than a week later that this same leader Ben, with half his men, rode into the camp site and asked to speak with the pastor. Pastor Joseph came out of the building expecting just about anything. The gang leader got of his horse and approached the pastor and reached out his hand and began to apologize.

He said that he and his men were very sorry for what they did and would the pastor be willing to teach them about this Jesus using the film they had heard about. Seeing the Lord's mighty hand in all this, the pastor smiled and asked the men to dismount and come into the church facility.

The band and its leader enjoyed the entire two-hour film. At the end this group of men asked if they could come back in a few days and learn more. Quickly the pastor sent a "thank you" heavenward and told the men they would be welcome and bring their families as well. This band leader, Ben, had some good training from pastor Joseph and has started his own church.

This house of worship also expanded and two more churches were planted. This is just one of the thousands of miracle stories the Jesus Film has written about it in its forty years of reports. I will share another one with you now. One of these stories is about a women visiting family in a city near her village and got a chance to receive Jesus as her Savior.

Excited and blessed she returned to her village and shared with friends and family what she had learned. A teacher in her village had one old torn up Bible to teach his small church. The believers in that village began to ask God for some Bibles. This man had the same dream twice, to be at a certain crossroad at the outside of his village at noon time the following Sunday.

One of our Campus Crusade's evangelism teams had loaded up their van with Bibles intending to smuggle them into one of the villages in that area. Each of these vans had a false floor built into the bottom which was loaded up with Bibles and these vans were always prayed over for the Holy Spirit to protect them.

At one of the checkpoints the drivers were forced to open the van and our two men ask God to blind the soldier's eyes. When our men opened the side doors of the van, the top of the Bibles could be seen, but as it happened at other times, the soldiers did not see the Bibles and told our men to go on their way, which of course they gratefully did.

Driving along, the van came close to a village when it suddenly stopped running and our men searched but could not find the reason for the breakdown. Suddenly they noticed a man sitting on a rock right by the crossroad and asked him if he could find the problem. The waiting Bible teacher could not find anything either but invited them to his home for some food and drink.

While talking, the man told about the villager's prayers for Bibles and our men stepped aside for a moment. They agreed that this was a sign from the Lord to leave the Bibles with these people and they would return home for more another time. Our men told the teacher about the Lord's plan to leave the Bibles for his village.

They said for him to get other villagers to unload the Bibles from the van and bring them in. Our men could not describe the joy and gratefulness of the villagers as they brought God's word into the house where they met to worship. This was also where they studied the Scriptures and they were praising God for His provision.

Many of them followed our men back to the crossroad where the van had broken down. A few of the villagers who knew about cars volunteered to check for the damage but could not find anything. After some prayer however, one of our men started the engine and it kicked in right away and showed that there was no damage.

The reason was clear, once again our awesome God had worked out His plans and without knowing had followed along. Our men were not surprised but the villagers could hardly contain their joy and kept thanking God, wanting to go back and spend time in those Bibles.

POLAND, THE OTHER PART OF MY DNA

Although I always knew that half of me is Polish, due to my Father and his family being from that country, I now found my thoughts on it. When I was younger it did not make a lot of difference to me because my mother was German and that is where I lived. It was not till I was in the US and became a Christian, that I began thinking about this part of my history.

Hearing in our JESUS Film reports some stories about the people of Poland and how this film was impacting their lives, I became interested. For some reason I began to think more and more about going over and learning about and seeing this part of my history. My work in the ministry of Campus Crusade for Christ had been for thirty-eight years in the department of the "Jesus Film Project."

This was a film God put on the heart of Dr. Bill Bright, the president of this ministry, who got in touch with a film producer. This producer worked with our man Paul Eshelman, who paid full attention to the accuracy of the Scriptures and the history of Israel. Not until then was the film produced by John Hayman and afterward released by Warner Bros. Studios.

Paul Eshelman then also oversaw and directed the distribution of the film into every country of the world. This God ordained film was released to the theaters all over the US and became very popular. This was now more than forty years ago and that blessed film has never lost it's popularity nor the number of Salvations the Lord has planned for it.

This far the JESUS film has been translated to more than 1,800 languages and was entirely filmed in the Holy Land, using the people who lived in these regions. The customs, clothing and foods were studied for two years before the film was made, desiring to be as true to the Bible as possible. It had also been produced in the Polish language and had some wonderful results in that country.

I was given a chance to live with one of our Campus Crusade staff families, so off I went to Poland. My melancholy emotions seemed strange to me until I realized it felt like I was back in the old part of Germany, in the years of my youth. We were working mostly with business women in this city and my partner and I met with women in large groups in different restaurants.

These ladies worked in the local businesses or had their own. We shared all the wonderful years of our ministry and the never-ending results of spending daily time in God's blessed word. The women had much interest in the intimate way we represented God and His desire for His children to love Him as He loves them.

We left with them some of the meaningful books Dr. Bill Bright, the president of Campus Crusade for Christ wrote and they were grateful. This is why it was more important to me than ever to be in His love letter. He never gets tired to reveal more of Himself and the awesome future He has for His children. My gratefulness to this faithful and patient God continues.

I remember that I was thirty-seven when I finally gave my life to Him and began to love Him back. What I have learned most is how valuable my daily time is in the Bible. Nothing could be more important to my Savior and to me than getting to know Him better. Because of this time in His Word, the Lord keeps Satan from leading me astray as often.

Instead God's Word guides me by continuing to show me that it is that truth which sets me free. Our precious God says in Ephesian 1:4 and 5, that He knew us and chose us before He made the world, then He adopted us into His family according to the good pleasure of His will. It can never be often enough that I tell my family and the youths I teach to take this valuable time.

This way they can prove that He Is always true to His promises. What He says will stand as it tells us in Psalm 33:9 "For He spoke and it was done, He commanded and it stood fast." And in verse :11 "The counsel of the Lord stands forever, the plans of His heart to all generations".

STILL MORE MINISTRY

On my way home from the Bible studies at Juvenile Hall I noticed a coffee shop with a lot of high school-aged kids hanging around. Immediately some One I love popped an opportunity into my head and the next day after work I visited there. The young people sat in groups of five or more and were in what seemed serious conversations.

Asking the Lord for courage, I approached the biggest of the groups and asked if they would mind my talking to them about God and His love for them. I could not believe that they were willing to meet with me and I sang all the way home. Starting with the largest of the groups I told them that I am a full- time missionary with a big Christian organization.

To my question if they would be interested in my stopping once or twice a week, I got a yes. I told them we could talk about who they thought God was and why He would love them. We agreed on the days I would be going to meet with them. Their questions and concerns came from their hearts and I wrote out some scriptures for them to study and one to memorize.

They loved being prayed for and little by little some admitted that their lives were changing as they started to read the Bibles I had given them. They admitted that not only did their grades go up but their relationships with their family members were improving. I could see our God drawing them close to Himself.

Using Joshua 1:8, and Psalms 1:1-3, I always show the youth I teach that the Lord promised meditating daily on His word would make them prosper and have good success in their lives. He goes on with telling them to be strong and courageous, not to be discouraged for the Lord their God will be with them wherever they go.

MORE ABOUT CAMP PENDLETON MINISTRY

I have shared that one of my grandsons joined the Marines and I told in my first book how I got started giving Bible studies there. It had turned out to be three nights a week, three hours each time on Camp Pendleton Marine Base. This became the most favorite of my ministries because I could take those of my young soldiers, who were off on the weekend, home with me.

My albums have many pictures of the floors in my living and dining room covered with young soldiers in sleeping bags. We were able to have some great times of prayer and studies in God's word as well as in my Church on Sundays. My Marines were grateful for their time with me because it kept them from going with most of the other guys to the nearby city for the weekend.

They would share with me their hurts and joys and they, as well as all my other students, loved being prayed for. All of them called me mom, they said I was their spiritual mom and it was a true blessing to me and helped me with my empty nest pain. My prayers and concerns were real as the Lord revealed to me their needs.

Some of my young soldiers said they joined the Marines to get away from their dysfunctional families. However all they found in the service was again someone telling them how bad and useless they are and that they would never amount to anything in this life. They did not realize until later that this was for their benefit. They needed to become sure of who they are and what they wanted out of life.

Many of those who were not believers in Jesus Christ made that decision in prayer at that time. We thanked the Lord for His perfect timing and we are waiting for Him to come and take us home. They were grateful to God that He had known this was the time for them. It was important that Satan could not put guilt on them about their past, he was not able to do this to me either.

One of the Marine Colonels wrote me a letter saying that he thanked God for sending me to his Marines to bring them the hope He promises His believers. He recommended me to other ministries as a volunteer because he had seen the change in some of his Marines after coming to the Bible studies. There were several of them ready to be kicked out of the Marines and be dishonorably discharged.

However, after coming a few times to the Bible studies, the Lord began to change their character and the leadership asked them to stay and one of them even finished his time with special honors. What a wonderful way to be used by God, not because I was perfect or had no faults but only because I had gathered up some courage and said "Here I am Lord, send me."

I used to ask the Lord to minimize my strong motherly feelings, since they were not needed so much now that my kids are gone from home. However, He just kept giving me more and more kids to love and be loved by, around 400 a month by now. The number of students change, especially in Juvenile Hall and at Camp Pendleton Marine Base. There is a 4 to 6 month turnaround where they move on to their next station.

There are dozens of farewell letters from these precious young men, thanking God for having me there for them. There are even a few letters from parents. One mom said in hers "since I knew my son was going in the Service I have been praying that the Lord would send him an angel and I thank God that He gave him you Hannah". Whenever Satan tries to get me down I pull out one or two of these letters and read them to him and he leaves.

Even my great grandchildren enjoy my teaching them what this faithful God has promised them, I wanted to be sure they would join me in heaven. When I started Bible study classes at their Grandpa's house, six of the ten were in high school, two were in junior high and two were in grade school.

Some of my great grands are now in the service, one is married and the younger ones I still see and teach. I thank my God every day for this great privilege. It is so important that we are that salt which Jesus talks about so we can preserve that awesome teaching our Lod gave us. We also need to make this precious word of God tasty and easy to understand.

It is important to show how real His love flows through every part of our lives. Also, that light of the world our God made us to be, is used so His Word can be shared with those seeking Him. My biggest joy has been their attention and one after another wanted to be baptized. What a blessing it is for me to know that they are saved and will not be left when Jesus comes to pick up those who believe in Him.

Seven of the great grandchildren, now all teens, I have taken to Wednesday night service, at the church their parents attend. The adults work that night, so by my taking them, their kids do not have to miss out and I enjoy the service as well. Any of the questions they had could be answered at our Monday night Bible study.

ANOTHER TRIP TO KENTUCKY

As you heard in my first book, my youngest son Bill and his wife Carol moved with their two children to Kentucky. I have been visiting them once a year, it was hard for me to change from seeing them every day. My daughter Lita took me to the airport again since she had taken me dozens of times for my overseas trips.

We arrived at the airport late because of extra heavy traffic and one of the freeway offramps had been closed. This turned out alright because my connecting flight had been canceled so they had to redirect me anyway. This time Bill and Carol had sent me the money for the flight and I was grateful because I did not have it.

Both parents took vacation and the kids were out of school so we had a great week together. We would rent a pontoon boat for one of the days to be on beautiful Lake Cumberland where the water is green and so clear you could see the bottom on most places.

These boats have a barbecue and ice chest on them and an upper deck with a slide into the water. That afternoon the weather predicted to have a heavy storm coming in toward evening. As we watched the black wall of clouds move closer, we planned to leave for home earlier than usual. We thought we had enough time, so we set up to barbecue our lunch.

Suddenly the bottom of the pit caught on fire and my level headed granddaughter Selena put it out with the Fire Extinguisher. We were grateful that at least one hot dog for each member was already cooked. We had just barely thrown out our fishing poles when it began to rain and none of us had brought a cover or umbrella so we got soaking wet.

Thanks to God it was not cold so none of us got sick. While my son Bill checked in the boat, I looked up the hill where the parking lot was located and asked the Lord how I was going to get up there with the ground so wet. That very moment a golf cart pulled up in front of me and a very nice gentleman and his wife asked if I would like to ride up the hill with them where the cars are.

I sent up a heartfelt thanks to my Lord and then thanked the couple. When we got closer to home the rain clouds had not arrived there yet and everything was still dry and Bill set up what was needed for the evening BBQ. Suddenly we realized that the huge black wall of clouds caught up after all and moved over us much faster than we had hoped till it covered us completely.

Just having learned about the power the Lord gives His children over His creation and some of the miracles a few of our Christian friends had experienced, I reacted. Confidently I said in a loud voice to the black cloud "we are not ready for you, you break up in Jesus name." A moment later we all looked up and that enormous cloud had broken into at least 20 or 30 small ones.

Everyone was totally amazed at the sight, the only shameful thing was that I was as surprised as they were, instead of bragging about our gracious God. The Lord talks about the authority He has given us in Luke 10:19 which says "I have given you authority to trample on snakes and scorpions and over all the power of the enemy and nothing will in any way harm you."

We are supposed to use that authority, but it takes trust in Him to really believe and do it. Slowly they all began to take our things inside, while Bill and I stayed out a little while longer. As we both went inside the first drops began to fall and after I closed the sliding door after us, it poured.

All of us had a good laugh afterwards and we said that we would try to pay more attention to God's promises in the scriptures, even in the daily situations. It is amazing how many thousands of promises and examples our Lord has written in His book for His children.

The next morning I got to sit face to face with my number twenty two great grandchild Jaxson, but since he had only seen me on the Messenger of the phone, he did not know what to do with me being there in person. It did not take him long to warm up to me and he liked spending time with his Oma.

He is the only one of my great grandchildren far away from me, all the other twenty one are close by for which I am grateful. Bill and Carol had become foster parents and I enjoyed meeting their two foster daughters. The girls were seventeen and eighteen and thanks to God's plan they both prayed to receive Christ as Lord and Savior with me and began to go to church with my son and his wife.

One of them turned eighteen shortly after I left and had to leave their home according to the rules laid down for them. However, with her Savior she had a new hope now and did not have to rely on the new people around her but in His faithfulness. Many of my own lessons came in some very unusual ways, and some of them came from the enemy.

However all of them, at the end, showed the Father's great love and protection. For instance, the only time my car ever broke down was on the way to do some Bible studies the Lord called me to give. One time it stopped in the middle of a major intersection on my way to give Bible study at Juvenile Hall. Two kind gentlemen pushed me over to the side of the road.

At my call, my son came to take me to the Youth Detention Center and picked me up after the lesson was done. When I got in my car and turned the key, it started up immediately and purred like a kitten showing that all was well with it. I realized that the enemy did not want me to teach God's holy Word.

Through these times I learned to trust in my faithful God and He always came through for me. After all, that is what the Bible promises and nothing is more precious to God than His children seeking Him and coming to know Him.

So many stories in the scriptures give us examples of believers being obedient to the Lord's commands. Then they are coming to know Him, getting greatly blessed and living in a life of joy. The Lord says in Joshuah 1:8 that we should meditate in His Word it day and night so we can do what is written therein. Then we shall prosper, then we shall have good success"

In Psalms 1:3 it says "Instead his delight is in the Word of the Lord and in it he meditates day and night. He is like a tree planted by the streams of water that bears its fruit in season and its leaves do not wither and whatever he does shall prosper". I can truly vouch for this Scripture because my Lord has so many times given or healed or guided me in unbelievable ways through His Word and just at the right time.

CONTINUING GROWTH

T his was not only because I learned about my God's love and faithfulness, but I also learned about the many tricks of my enemy. The Lord tells in Ephesians 6:16 that as a believer I can put those fiery darts Satan throws at me out, by my strong faith. That faith I find by being daily in that blessed Word my God has written for me to follow and believe in.

Faith is just believing in what He has promised, even if I can not see it yet. Learning early that trials are mostly tools my beloved Lord allows to bring me to perfection, it caused me to do a lot less complaining and whining. In 1Corinthians 10:13, He promised that He would never give me more than I could handle and even then He would give me a way of escape.

So instead of whining again I learned to ask "what am I to do with this Lord?" even if I did not like it and in His faithful way He always showed me. The things I learned and I began to teach my students was that the Lord says in His word "The power of life and death is in the tongue" and it shocked them.

Having heard so many of the youth, on Camp Pendleton and the city schools and in Juvenile Hall use not only bad language but also cut each other down, I reacted. Quickly I put together a Bible study to show them that this is very displeasing to God. He never puts us down and it hurts Him when we do it to others, an encouraging word can be such a blessing and bring healing.

Recalling the times I have been deeply hurt by someone's words and I have done the same to someone else, I pleaded with the Holy Spirit for help and began to depend on His faithfulness. I asked Him to Convict me when I am about to say something hurtful instead of making me aware after I already said it.

Starting to spend time in God's wonderful word twice a day, the blessings came in many different ways. One of them was by my ministries increasing in the young people who came to participate. They were bringing me joy in the way they better listened and goofing around less. Sometimes I even got to see them be kind to some one else.

Once in a while they totally surprised me by giving up something they like to somebody who needed it. There is just is no way for me to describe the rewards I have experienced or the many testimonies I have heard that came from being obedient to God's Word. The Scriptures tell us that obedience is more important to God than sacrifice.

THE POWER OF PRAYER

L earning how much our God loves it when we remind Him of His promises, I began to use Scriptures in my prayers. My favorite one was to remind Him of what He promised in regards to drawing my children and all I prayed for close to Him in:

Isiah 55:10 which says: "as the rain and snow come down from heaven and do not return to it without watering the earth and making it bud and flourish so that it yields seeds for the sower and bread for the eater, so shall My word be that comes forth from My mouth, it will not return to Me empty, but it will accomplish what I desire and achieve the purpose for which I sent it."

Believing with all my heart that He sent His precious Word for salvation, I claimed it for my children and their mates, my grandchildren and their mates and my great grandchildren, knowing that my beloved God would answer. Longing with all my heart for them and others I pray for, not just to know God but be in love with Him.

I lift up the ones I pray for before my Savior God as often as they came to my mind, and that is often. Nothing would change their lives as being in love with Him, I know that from my own experience. Being in love with my Savior truly changed my live. Knowing that this awesome Creator not only hears my prayers but He answers them.

SEARCH FOR ME AND YOU WILL FIND ME

L ook at my salvation, I was not looking for God but He had scheduled that special day a long time ago. Convinced that the Lord would not bother with me because I had not been to church or taken any interest in Him, I was sure that I was totally on my own with my pain and loneliness. However, after He saved my children and I, we found out that He knew us and chose us a very long time ago.

It was humbling to me and caused my love for Him to increase greatly. Especially when He tells us in Ephesians 1:4 and 5, that He chose us in Jesus before the foundation of the world, to be holy and blameless in His sight. Our Lord says that in love He predestined us to be adopted through Jesus Christ for Himself according to His pleasure and will.

It just caused me to cry when I tried to imagine how long and lovingly He has waited for me to come into His waiting arms. This made me see my childhood and teen-age years in a whole different light. Most of all His awesome protection over my mom, my two sisters and me before the end of the war in Germany.

One time the protection was from a huge bomb that hit the ground on the other side of a cellar wall we were sitting against. We were all thrown to the ground, the walls and ceilings crumbled and the electricity went out. We all screamed and after making sure there was no more, using our flashlights we found our way home.

The following morning our grandpa took us children to the outside of that wall we were sitting against the previous night. To our shock, there was this enormous hole in the ground with a very large black bomb in it which had not exploded. When the bomb squad arrived and chased us away, my grandpa heard them say to each other this **monster** would have wiped out at least thirty or forty of these apartment complexes.

This was only one of many times our God protected us. Our loving Lord knew that some day we would receive Him and walk with Him in His blessed way. This began to show me the truth about God knowing all about us long before it happens. Like He says in Psalm 139 :16 that He saw my unformed body and all the days ordained for me were written in His book before one of them came to be. Wow, He knew all about me and still loved me.

WALKING IN HIS WAY AND GROWING

Little by little I began to like myself and not always look at the things I had not conquered yet and I listened less to the enemy's accusations. It also helped me to be less offended by others critical opinions. Instead I thought more about what my Savior said, that I am cleansed, forgiven and on my way home. Before Jesus went back up to the Father, He promised to be preparing a place for His believers. Then He would come to get them, that where He is they will be also.

This is one of His greatest promises and it has helped me though many trials. Being so easily offended came when it was about something I knew I was not perfect in yet, even though I tried. Handling criticism for things my beloved God had already improved helped me to be patient and pray for the gossipers to receive His help also.

It was in my daily times in God's word I began to learn more and more that this truth which He promised, would set me free. His love set me free from so many things that had plagued me before my salvation and used to make my life unhappy. This also truly set me free from all the lies and superstition I grew up in and no one had the courage to correct them.

So I lived like all others around me in fear of everything I could not see. It made me lose out on many things that would have led me to the truth of God much sooner. I also could have found that indescribable Salvation at a much earlier time. My friend Webster says that "courage is the secret sauce that allows you to act despite your fears and take the first step".

This led me finally to reject my fears more and remind myself daily of His awesome promises. It also made me seek this God, who had given Himself in the most painful and degrading death, with my whole heart. Now this freedom started to become reality and one of the ways was by less fear of Satan and His helpers.

Realizing that in one of my favorite scriptures, Luke 10:19 my Savior says "Behold, I have given you authority to tread upon serpents and scorpions, and over all the power of the enemy, and nothing shall in any wise hurt you". WOW, this greatly decreased my living in fear of this enemy whom Jesus defeated by His blood.

THE WONDER AND LIFE CHANGING WAY OF FORGIVENESS

This was the first lesson my awesome Lord had caused me to learn, because I could not be in close fellowship with Him while I had something against people who had hurt me. Donna, the young lady from Campus Crusade for Christ, who had led me to the Lord, paid for me to attend a Bill Gothard Seminar.

This teaching was mostly about forgiveness and I attended while this new sister in Christ watched my kids. In my first book I shared that my husband of fifteen years left our four children and me and moved in with a young girl. This brought unbelievable pain and sorrow to my girls and me.

The boys are each 10 years younger than the girls so this all did not affect them much yet. After Jesus entered my heart and life, He enabled me to forgive, but the pain still hit sometimes, especially when I saw my children's father with his girlfriend.

This "Bill Gothard Seminar" left a deep impression on me. I chose to be obedient, figuring to start with the hardest, my ex-husband Bill. Taking a deep breath, I began to dial his number, hoping he would not answer, but he did. So, I asked him to forgive me for what I did for him to stop loving me. Smartly he said "if it makes you feel good, yea I forgive you."

This aroused some anger in me and I thought "Who forgives whom here?" This attitude I had to immediately confess to the Lord. The other two were easier and both said that they were not aware that they had hurt me, which I could not believe. However, after I was done, the reward of having been obedient was a sweet feeling of peace.

The whole matter faded in the background where it belonged. The healing could not have taken place without forgiveness and that is one of my favorite subjects to teach my young people, especially those I counsel and teach in Juvenile Hall. When God says in Roman 12:19 "Vengeance is Mine, I will repay."

Our lord means He does not want us to get even with people who have hurt or cheated us. Explaining to them that when they get even by themselves, the other person does not admit that he is wrong, he gets back at him. That becomes a vicious circle that God does not want them to be in.

Instead it is better to leave the vengeance to the Lord who can do it without them being accused of doing someone harm. I learned there is always a blessing for obedience and the heart always feels a wonderful release and freedom. When I use this in my Bible studies I make them aware of what I have learned myself early.

This is, that closeness with this God of love is not possible while there is a grudge against anyone in my heart. The Lord says in "Matthew 5:23 if you are bringing an offering to the altar and you remember that your brother has something against you, leave the offering and first be reconciled with your brother" This is very important to the Lord

TRULY A NEW CREATION?

It took a long time for me for me not to compare myself with other people hoping I would become like them or could have the same talents or growth. It convicted me that I was telling my Savior that He made a mistake in my creation. More than anything I wanted my beloved bridegroom to be pleased because He did so much for me just so I could be His for all eternity.

To have the right feelings and attitudes meant a lot to me but I still messed up. I had to admit that the old me came less and less to the surface by being twice daily in God's precious Word. Learning that the Lord knew the moment I would surrender my life fully into His waiting hands, I just wept. It would take a much greater love than I can imagine for Him to wait so long for this moment to arrive.

Longing to know this God deeper, I increased my time in His blessed word and my knowledge of Him grew. It began a journey that I hope will never end, in spite of my still imperfect character. He has promised to never leave or forsake me, this means His eyes are always on me, guiding me. I took that promise very seriously especially in my many overseas trips where no harm ever came to me.

ONE OF THE AWESOME CHRISTIAN GATHERINGS

A powerful program of many Christian Churches in Germany, called "Christival", had 34,000 students sign up from all over Europe but 38,000 arrived. The most awesome testimonies about our Savior were reported. This took place in the largest city in East Germany, Dresden. However, there were not enough hotels and churches to house the extra 4,000. So, the businesses in this city offered them their conference rooms and all had housing.

After morning service I was allowed to share my testimony with salvation at The Jesus Project booth, which was well attended. In the afternoon we set up tables and served coffee and cookies to visitors and shared the "Four Spiritual Laws" by Dr. Bill Bright with them and many received Jesus as their Lord and Savior. At 5:00pm daily, all 38,000 students and us volunteers met at East Germany's largest football stadium for worship and powerful messages by different well-known speakers.

My tears just flowed when these students raised their hands and sang Maranatha songs, many recorded in the U.S. and we spent an hour each night worshiping Jesus. Each night a large number of these students met at the beach to dance and have fellowship, often with students from other countries and they would share ways of worship in their churches.

The newspapers gave beautiful stories praising the good behavior of these students and their respectful attitudes toward the elderly and each other. We were told that the West German students had raised funds so the students from East Germany could also attend. Never could I tell of all the blessings and the salvations that took place in this awesome conference.

Only our beloved Savior knows, but the joys and rewards He gave to us and we will never forget God's great faithfulness. Our Jesus Project team consisted of 3 Americans, two Turks, 2 Chinese and two Russians. We were able to spent those 8 days with other Campus Crusade Staff who lived and ministered in Dresden.

SO MANY ANSWERED PRAYERS

Having lost close connection with a friend by her getting married, I asked my beloved Lord to please send me another one and of course He answered. At the invitation to a ladies luncheon, while standing in line a lady behind me introduced herself. When I mentioned that I liked the soft music they were playing at this luncheon she said she played the harp.

She explained that she had just finished a CD and offered for me to buy last one she had. When I do my writings or prepare my Bible studies, I need music without words so I bought one from her. I don't remember how we got to our nationalities but she said that being from Switzerland she spoke perfect German.

At this I laughed and replied that I spoke it also, at that we hugged and we just clicked. This way God answered my prayer and a lovely friendship began. This friendship grew when we discovered that we both were in love with our God and loved speaking with Him and about Him.

We discovered also that we were both free on Fridays and so we would spend those days together. We also like the same food and love the same kind of music. Thank you Lord! There have been many ways that we have been able to help and complete each other.

However, the best thing is that we are both in love with Jesus and we thank him for all the little things He does for us. Almost every night we would call each other for a good night prayer. Before we separate we always pray and thank God for bringing us together and thank Him for His protection.,

His faithfulness is indescribable. One night we attended Wednesday evening service at her church and each of us had the chance to minister to different people who were in spiritual need My young man had just been told that he was not good in praying and was crying. I told him that at sixteen was a great time to start and the Lord would keep adding to that.

Encouraging him not to give up but to begin reading God's Word every day and his prayer language would develop. This would also help him to start hearing the voice of this God of love and assure him that he is in His presence every moment. My friend and I left the church blessed that our beloved God was able to use us for someone.

HIS PROTECTION IS AWESOME AND CONSTANT

After I had given my life to the Lord I remembered all the times the Lord had protected my children and me in our many outdoor trips, especially up and down the mountains. My life became like a big adventure, never knowing what tomorrow would bring. Yet I believed with all my heart that He would keep His many promises.

As it says in Romans 8:28 "We know that all things work together for good to those who love God, to those who are the called according to His purpose". My greatest responsibility was raising my four children in the knowledge of God. However, when they were gone, the girls were married and the boys in the Service, the Lord began to send me all over the world.

I loved seeing so much of His awesome creation and fell in love with many places. Never having imagined to be in these beautiful countries, my mind expanded greatly. It gave me a whole new vision and reasons for prayer. There developed a deep longing to be used by my God for these precious people to be saved from their enemy, just like I was.

Never did I imagine to be writing a book, but I always longed to leave something behind when the Lord would take me home. It would have to be something that would glorify this unique and awesome God I came to know. I wanted something that would tell them that He is not the powerful judge who makes us suffer for everything we have done wrong, as I was told.

We never knew how He feels about us until after death when He tells us, in front of everyone else, what we have done wrong and where we are going to spend eternity. This is why the assurance of salvation is so very precious to me because I have the choice where I spend my eternal life. God clearly reveals both sides of the eternal plan to us and we can choose.

By my seeking Him or rejecting Him, I can choose where I want to spend eternal life, with Him or with my enemy. What an awesome freedom that gives because, even though not yet perfect, I stand before my heavenly Father clean and forgiven. Jesus says in His prayer to the Father in John, chapter 17 many times "I am in them and they are in Me,"

ANOTHER KENTUCKY AND COLORADO VISIT

P lanning this trip was special because after Kentucky I would fly to Colorado for Campus Crusades bi-yearly staff training which I love so much. My now 43 years with this blessed ministry have been continuous joy, learning and growth. Each meeting meant seeing bosses and co-workers from times gone by.

We would worship our beloved God in such meaningful ways, our own music teams using their great talents to lead us. I could have sworn each morning that the big "Moby Gym" raised off the ground from our worship. The gym was called Moby because it was in shape of a big whale. Our staff training took place at the beautiful Colorado State College in July of every other year.

The college was big enough to handle all 5000 plus of our U.S. staff, the rest of our staff are in every country of the world. Those ten days always go by too fast with the awesome worship and popular speakers and precious fellowship. Each of the classes were on different subjects so we could choose what would help and minister to us the best.

The children had their own classes and lunch during the day, they enjoyed that and the parents were able to listen well to the different speakers. These staff-kids received also good Bible teaching, heathy lunches and were together with their parents for the evening. At that time there were usually concerts from different Christian entertainment groups.

So once again I purchased my tickets early and packed last minute, having done it for dozens of overseas trips. This way I know just what I need for which season and which country. My daughter Christy always takes good care of my Manufactured home and my gardener does a great job with my yard and 5 fruit trees.

There have never been any problems in my 13 years here in this park, even though it is a family park. Just two weeks absence, what could happen, this was not my first absence? Happily boarding my flight on July 11, I looked forward to my once-a-year visit to my youngest son Bill and his great family which I love.

With Lita taking me to the airport as she usually does, I had no concerns, I love flying. My Hope is always to have a non-believing neighbor so I can share with them about a loving God having changed the lives of my children and me and He could do the same thing for them if they would ask Him.

There is nothing no greater joy and blessing than leading someone to my Savior knowing from experience what He will do for their lives. On the flight to Kentucky I had two chances to share about the faithful God I believe in. One was a Christian sister and we enjoyed praising God for His work in our lives.

After changing planes, the gentleman next to me said that he did not believe that there is a God. Sharing the reason for my flight and asking for the reason for his, I told him that I was made a single mom of our four children and after not wanting to continue living, God arranged a way for me to know Him.

Continuing with how this God I believe in had turned our lives from very painful to a life of great hope he began to listen. Taking out a Four Spiritual Laws booklet I asked him to read it when he had a chance. To my surprise he began to read it right then and continued till our plane landed, at which time he put it in his back pocket and wished me a pleasant day.

I prayed that God would make a new beginning in his life. There have been so many ways to introduce someone to this awesome Savior and each time was a little different. It was always a joy to see what person and subject the Lord would choose.

Bill and his wife Carol were anxiously waiting for me and had brought 2 1/2 year old Jaxson with them, my number 22 great grandchild, making it a lively ride home. One of our yearly boat rides on Lake Cumberland had been planned and as usual it included the members of the household plus me.

We had packed everything needed for a nice barbecue with potato salad and various chips and drinks and we were ready for some fishing again. None of us caught anything but we left early enough to miss the rain and when we got home we were tired but relaxed.

We had no adventure this time realizing that we usually don't do our trips in a boring fashion. This evening we skipped the bonfire and the beloved s'mores. We knew we had four more days before I would leave for Colorado so we stayed in and played games.

THE MOST PAINFUL
ADVENTURE OF MY LIFE

While visiting in Kentucky, a relative and close friend of the family and sweet sister in Christ had invited me out to lunch. We wanted to spend some time together and catch up on what God had done in our lives. It was a joyful time of praising our loving God and laughing at His great sense of humor.

It is always a blessing to be together with this sister because we both felt free to have conversations about this awesome Lord who saved us from the fires of hell. Instead He has suffered greatly to give us eternal life with Him in the most beautiful place we could ever imagine. It was a blessing not to have to worry that anyone thought us to be fanatical.

After we were done, we pulled in my son's driveway for her to drop me off, when suddenly there was a tremendous impact and noise on the right side of the car where I was sitting. An overwhelming pain ran through the right side of my body as I was crunched together in my car seat. I also had trouble breathing and realized that we were hit by a car.

There was no more awareness of anything until I heard a fire engine and an ambulance arrive. Realizing that I was totally covered with hundreds of small pieces of glass and the pain was increasing I could not help but scream. The two firemen closest to me said "mahm we have to cut your dress open on the left side so we can roll all that glass of you".

The pain on the right side of my body and my chest was so great I could not have cared less what they were doing. They covered me with a blanked and said "mahm, we can only get you out of your seat if we slide you down and onto our gurney." This was the last thing I remembered until I was in the ambulance with an IV in each arm.

Having always been concerned what I would do if something terrible would happen to me, I was blessed hearing myself praising my beloved God the whole drive. Because they used the lights and the sirens on the ambulance, the 1 ½ hour drive to the hospital in Lexington, the ride was cut to 45 minutes.

The pain was unbearable as they lifted me from the gurney to the X-ray table, then to the MRI bar, then to the cot and finally on a bed. All I could do was cry and call on the Lord Jesus. Each time that four people were lifting me in a sheet, they were crushing my broken body together. They informed me that my pelvis was broken in three places and needs instant surgery.

They continued to inform me that I have a dozen fractured ribs, eight of them in my right upper body and four on my left side. An immediate surgery was done to repair the three brakes in my Pelvis using scews to bring my hip back up where it belonged. I was given more pain medication and something for sleep.

The first month I spent in UK Chandler Hospital under excellent care, with dozens of nurses and aides in prayer for me because these staff were changed around every three days. Some of them bought my book that is for sale in many Christian-book-stores but easiest and fastest from Amazon. These precious staff said they love it that I always have Christian music on.

Telling them that I wrote the book under my birth name "Hofer" not under Casarez, they said they were blessed by it and shared it with others. There were especially sweet hours with my beloved Lord and Savior like I never had before and my love for Him greatly deepened. One of my favorite teachers says "God will give you overcoming strength in overwhelming moments."

One thing that made my pain easier was the joy that both my sons spend the first four days and nights with me, they got permission to sleep on couches in my room. Steve took those days off from work and came from South Carolina and Bill also got 4 days off from work and he continued visiting every day after work.

My girls, grandchildren, great grandchildren and friends called almost every day to check on me and to assure me of their love and prayers. One thing I have always been concerned about was what I would do when I was in real trouble or great pain, would I doubt my Lord or turn from Him. I was so relieved and grateful when I heard myself not doubting His great love for me.

For my second month I was transferred to Lake Cumberland Regional Hospital which is in Somersett and has the whole third floor as physical therapy. I was placed in a room on the third floor and it was only a fifteen minute drive from my son Bill's house, which made his daily visits easier than the long rides before.

Physical Therapy wasn't easy but it's easier now and I can feel the benefit of it. I know I will be walking again. Both my doctors, in Kentucky and the ones in California, when seeing my X-rays said "I can't believe you are alive" and my walking again was doubtful.

The way the accident happened was so unusual, it showed that my enemy wanted me out of the Lord's work, but my Father said NO. We had pulled into my son's driveway when a 17-year old women, coming on the left side of the street, instead of passing behind us turned right into the lawn and into our car.

The police said that there were no marks that the girl even hit the brakes, she came full speed. The fire team who freed me out of my seat was the team my son belongs to, who is also a fireman in his town. My granddaughter took pictures of the car after the ambulance took me.

The firemen and every one who saw the pictures agreed that if that car had hit ours just one foot further to the front I would never walk again. it would have crushed both my hips and my whole Pelvis and I would never have walked again. Knowing that this was my Fathers choice, I said a sincere prayer of thanksgiving to my beloved God.

Even though God allowed the accident, He saved me from death, because not just my body would have been destroyed. The side frame of the door was hanging over my head and would have gone into my head. I give my testimony at my church and other places. I show the pictures of the car so they can see what could have happened and they thank God for His mercy on me.

Trusting my beloved Lord, I did not need to ask Him to show me the purpose of this happening. By now He has shown me His faithfulness in so many ways and He is the same yesterday, today and forever. At the point of my salvation I had no job, no car and no will to live but my Lord knew already how this would change.

He knew how much beauty and purpose He would bring into the lives of my children and me. He also had in His plan how many more would enter His kingdom because He saved me from an eternity in hell and separation from His loving arms forever. He knew that I would be obedient to His will, even when it was not always easy or comfortable.

I can't even imagine how many times my loving God has kept harm and death from me and told the enemy "no" or "only this far" and how often He turned something meant for bad and worked it into something good like He promises in Romans 8:38. Just like this last adventure, it has brought me an even deeper understanding of His love for me. I look forward for Him showing me His molding of my future even though the doctors could not believe I was alive and were not sure I would walk again.

Since I healed, some great blessings have already come into my life and I am so grateful to my God. One of them is that He has given me two more schools to give Bible studies in. Another is that I have joined a ministry called "THE JOY COMPANY, a ministry to schools." In this I can work with 15 high school students who are the leaders in their school's Christian club.

We meet twice a week and have a beautiful fellowship and text each other often. By the way, I am walking! Praise God!!!! Almost all schools in the counties in my area have these clubs and these young leaders take them serious. These high schoolers want to do a good job for the Lord so they come to the Bible classes.

Their desire to serve the Lord pleases His heart even more than us teachers. In Psalm 32:8 "I will instruct you and teach you the way you should go, I will guide you with My eye on you." He has never let down with this promise I have always totally depended on my Lord for this.

Another blessing from this car accident is that I received a settlement from the insurance companies which paid part of my tremendous hospital bills. These hospital bills came to more than $200,000.- but my part of this was $2,485.- which amazes me. God has always taken care of me and has blessed those He used to help me in many different ways and they always knew it was from the Lord.

Many times I have asked my beloved Savior to release me from the payments of my home and car but I could not imagine how He would do this. The Bible says that we should not owe anybody anything even though a home and a car are really necessities. Also I had one small loan that I was ashamed of because I did not wait for the Lord to advise or supply but went ahead and borrowed the money.

But in His love He took care of this too. My sweet daughter-in-law hired a lawyer after my car accident and informed me afterwards. I had no idea that you can do this, this was my first accident. To my surprise and gratefulness, eight month later, they sent me a settlement and it was enough to pay off my Home, my car and that loan.

This money came in at the same time my paycheck was cut in half due to sixteen of my precious supporters going home to be with the Lord in one year. They were all in their nineties and I miss them, but we get to spend eternity with our beloved Lord and each other.

The precious young student leaders in the Joy Company enjoy using God's Word to explain how living this Christian live is possible. They are also available after classes to meet with anyone who has questions or need help. Several are planning to go into ministry, maybe even overseas.

The Pastor and I will get them in touch with organizations like Campus Crusade for Christ that have ministries in other countries. What a reward to have a part in these young missionaries' work by contributing and teaching them as they seek the lost. It is such a blessing that the Lord can use Pastor Devo and me to love and guide these young missionaries.

On the top of my prayer letters to my supporters I have the picture of an eagle and Isiah 40:31 "those who wait on the Lord shall renew their strength, they shall mount up with wings like eagles they shall run and not get weary, they shall walk and not faint."

This is why I love the song that says "I can fly higher than an eagle because you {Jesus) are the wind beneath my wings". It makes me cry when I think where my children and I would be had this great God not saved us.

There has been another, very recent healing in my life. One pain that was in my left shoulder since the car accident a year ago was not bad. There was so much damage on the right side where the car hit us that no one, including me, paid much attention to it. However, in the meantime the pain got worse and I had to take more and more pain pills.

I intended to see my orthopedic doctor but things came up and I was afraid what he would say. A week ago, I was turning in bed and there was a snap in my shoulder and the pain was severe. It was impossible for me to use my arm to get up or even raise the arm at all. I called my doctor and he agreed to see me as soon as he got in the office.

After a series of x-rays he showed me the problem and stated "it is really bad Hannah, the only way this can be helped is by replacing your whole shoulder joint". He continued "I am setting up a cat scan and make an appointment with a shoulder specialist who will do the surgery."

I came home, after my daughter had taken me to this appointment, since I could not drive, I laid down on my bed to relieve the pain. My bad shoulder is the left one and without thinking I was laying my phone on the left side of my bed. Suddenly the phone rang and I quickly reached to answer with my left hand, when I suddenly realized that there was no pain.

Dropping the phone without answering, I raised my arm way up and down again, then moved it to the extreme right, then to the left. With tears of joy I turned my arm round and round like a baseball player and with absolutely no pain. Joyfully I ran into the living room to show my son and daughter the miracle and we laughed and kept praising our beloved God.

Informing all my family, friends and co- workers was such a joy because they all rejoiced with me and thanked our merciful Lord for His healing touch. I will keep you informed why this awesome God has kept me alive and He has already given me ideas for a third book. He says He knows the plans He has for me and they are for good, not for evil.

This gives me true peace because as He promised us there is no one and nothing that can ever separate us from His love. (Romans 8:38 and 39) which says that neither death nor life, neither demons or angels, nor powers, nor things present nor things to come, nor depth, nor any other created thing, shall be able to separate us from the love of God which is in Christ Jesus our Lord.

My Lord has blessed me so I could be a blessing to others. He made my life into an example of His compassion and never-ending love for His children, not forgetting His protection, even though I need work yet.

There is one more big trial that has just entered the lives of my family and me. On September 15 this year, my precious 26-year-old grandson went to be with the Lord. He had been away from God for a few years. However a week before his death he came to his Father and told him he wanted to have Bible studies with him again.

They had their first study in my house, which lasted about three hours and Steven wanted more. Two days later his dad and he went ocean fishing and his dad told me that all Steven wanted to talk about was the Lord. When I heard about Stevens homegoing it greatly eased my mourning being sure I will see him again when I join him in heaven.

It was the same when my beautiful, 18 year old granddaughter Ericka, was killed in an accident eight years ago. Three day before her death she called me and said "Oma, I went to church with my friend and after the service I went forward and gave my life back to the Lord, I will come to church with you again.

I could never describe my love for my God for easing my grief by letting me know that there are two more beloved family members who are waiting for me to come home also. There is no way for me to tell of this indescribable heart of this God of love. My knowledge of Him is still too limited. This God, with great longing, has waited for all His children to be with Him since He began it all.

There is one more encouraging word from one of my blessed teachers, that I say almost every morning, "Whatever I focus on will grow in me and whatever grows in me, I will become."

My prayer is that He will never stop using me no matter where I am or what I am doing in this life.

THE FOUR SPIRITUAL LAWS

The Spirit-filled Life

Every day can be an exciting adventure for the Christian who knows the reality of being filled with the Holy Spirit and who lives constantly, moment by moment, under His gracious direction.

The Bible tells us that there are three kinds of people:

1. **Natural Man:** One who has not received Christ.

Self-Directed Life

S – Self is on the throne

† – Christ is outside the life

● – Interests are directed by self, often resulting in discord and frustration

"A natural man does not accept the things of the Spirit of God; for they are foolishness to him, and he cannot understand them, because they are spiritually appraised" (1 Corinthians 2:14, NASB).

Christ-Directed Life

S – Christ is in the life and on the throne

† – Self is yielding to Christ

● – Interests are directed by Christ, resulting in harmony with God's plan

2. **Spiritual Man:** One who is directed and empowered by the Holy Spirit.

"He who is spiritual appraises all things" (1 Corinthians 2:15, NASB).

3. **Carnal Man**: One who has received Christ, but who lives in defeat because he trusts in his own efforts to live the Christian life.

Self-Directed Life

S – Self is on the throne

† – Christ dethroned and not allowed to direct the life

● – Interests are directed by self, often resulting in discord and frustration

"I, brethren, could not speak to you as to spiritual people but as to carnal, as to babes in Christ. I fed you with milk and not with solid food; for until now you were not able to receive it, and even now you are still not able; for you are still carnal. For when there are envy, strife, and divisions among you, are you not carnal and behaving like mere men?" (1 Corinthians 3:1–3).

The following are four principles for living the Spirit-filled life:

1 God has provided for us an abundant and fruitful Christian life.

"Jesus said, 'I have come that they may have life, and that they may have it more abundantly'" (John 10:10, NKJ).

"The fruit of the Spirit is love, joy, peace, patience, kindness, goodness, faithfulness, gentleness, self-control; against such things there is no law" (Galatians 5:22,23).

Read John 15:5 and Acts 1:8.

The following are some personal traits of the spiritual man that result from trusting God:

- Love
- Joy
- Peace
- Patience
- Kindness
- Faithfulness
- Goodness

- Life is Christ-centered
- Empowered by Holy Spirit
- Introduces others to Christ
- Has effective prayer life
- Understands God's Word
- Trusts God
- Obeys God

The degree to which these traits are manifested in the life depends on the extent to which the Christian trusts the Lord with every detail of his life, and on his maturity in Christ. One who is only beginning to understand the ministry of the Holy Spirit should not be discouraged if he is not as fruitful as more mature Christians who have known and experienced this truth for a longer period.

Why is it that most Christians are not experiencing the abundant life?

2 Carnal Christians cannot experience the abundant and fruitful Christian life.

The carnal man trusts in his own efforts to live the Christian life:

- He is either uninformed about, or has forgotten, God's love, forgiveness, and power (Romans 5:8–10; Hebrews 10:1–25; 1 John 1; 2:1–3; 2 Peter 1:9).
- He has an up-and-down spiritual experience.
- He wants to do what is right, but cannot.
- He fails to draw on the power of the Holy Spirit to live the Christian life (1 Corinthians 3:1–3; Romans 7:15–24; 8:7; Galatians 5:16–18).

Some or all of the following traits may characterize the carnal man— the Christian who does not fully trust God:

- Legalistic attitude
- Impure thoughts
- Jealousy
- Guilt
- Worry
- Discouragement
- Critical spirit
- Frustration

- Aimlessness
- Fear
- Ignorance of his spiritual heritage
- Unbelief
- Disobedience
- Loss of love for God and for others
- Poor prayer life
- No desire for Bible study

(The individual who professes to be a Christian but who continues to practice sin should realize that he may not be a Christian at all, according to 1 John 2:3; 3:6–9; and Ephesians 5:5.)

The third truth gives us the only solution to this problem...

3 Jesus promised the abundant and fruitful life as the result of being filled (directed and empowered) by the Holy Spirit.

The Spirit-filled life is the Christ-directed life by which Christ lives His life in and through us in the power of the Holy Spirit (John 15).

- One becomes a Christian through the ministry of the Holy Spirit (John 3:1–8.) From the moment of spiritual birth, the Christian is indwelt by the Holy Spirit at all times (John 1:12; Colossians 2:9,10; John 14:16,17).

  All Christians are indwelt by the Holy Spirit, but not all Christians are filled (directed, controlled, and empowered) by the Holy Spirit on an ongoing basis.

- The Holy Spirit is the source of the overflowing life (John 7:37–39).

- In His last command before His ascension, Christ promised the power of the Holy Spirit to enable us to be witnesses for Him (Acts 1:1–9).

How, then, can one be filled with the Holy Spirit?

4 We are filled (directed and empowered) by the Holy Spirit by faith; then we can experience the abundant and fruitful life that Christ promised to each Christian.

You can appropriate the filling of the Holy Spirit right now if you:

- Sincerely desire to be directed and empowered by the Holy Spirit (Matthew 5:6; John 7:37–39).

- Confess your sins. By faith, thank God that He has forgiven all of your sins—past, present, and future—because Christ died for you (Colossians 2:13–15).

- Present every area of your life to God (Romans 12:1,2).

- By faith claim the fullness of the Holy Spirit, according to:

  His command: Be filled with the Spirit. "Do not get drunk on wine, which leads to debauchery. Instead, be filled with the Spirit" (Ephesians 5:18).

His promise: He will always answer when we pray according to His will. "This is the confidence we have in approaching God: that if we ask anything according to his will, he hears us. And if we know that He hears us—whatever we ask—we know that we have what we asked of Him" (1 John 5:14,15).

How to Pray in Faith to be Filled With the Holy Spirit

We are filled with the Holy Spirit by faith alone. However, true prayer is one way of expressing your faith. The following is a suggested prayer:

Dear Father, I need You. I acknowledge that I have been directing my own life and that, as a result, I have sinned against You. I thank You that You have forgiven my sins through Christ's death on the cross for me. I now invite Christ to again take His place on the throne of my life. Fill me with the Holy Spirit as You commanded me to be filled, and as You promised in Your Word that You would do if I asked in faith. I pray this in the name of Jesus. As an expression of my faith, I now thank You for directing my life and for filling me with the Holy Spirit.

Does this prayer express the desire of your heart? If so, bow in prayer and trust God to fill you with the Holy Spirit right now.

HAVE YOU HEARD OF THE FOUR SPIRITUAL LAWS?

Just as there are physical laws that govern the physical universe, so are there spiritual laws, which govern your relationship with God.

LAW 1. GOD LOVES YOU AND OFFERS A WONDERFUL PLAN FOR YOUR LIFE.

God's Love
"God so loved the world that He gave His one and only Son, that whoever believes in Him shall not perish, but have eternal life" (John 3:16 NIV).

God's Plan
[Christ speaking] "I came that they might have life, and might have it abundantly" [that it might be full and meaningful] (John 10:10).

Why is it that most people are not experiencing the abundant life? Because...

LAW 2. MAN IS SINFUL AND SEPARATED FROM GOD. THEREFORE, HE CANNOT KNOW
AND EXPERIENCE GOD'S LOVE AND PLAN FOR HIS LIFE.

Man Is Sinful
"All have sinned and fall short of the glory of God" (Romans 3:23).

Man was created to have fellowship with God; but, because of his stubborn self-will, he chose to go his own independent way, and fellowship with God was broken. This self-will, characterized by an attitude of active rebellion or passive indifference, is an evidence of what the Bible calls sin.

Man Is Separated
"The wages of sin is death" [spiritual separation from God] (Romans 6: 23).

This diagram illustrates that God is holy and man is sinful. A great gulf separates the two. The arrows illustrate that man is continually trying to reach God and the abundant life through his own efforts, such as a good life, philosophy, or religion—but he inevitably fails.

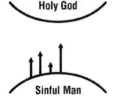

Holy God

Sinful Man

The third law explains the only way to bridge this gulf...

LAW 3. JESUS CHRIST IS GOD'S ONLY PROVISION FOR MAN'S SIN.
THROUGH HIM YOU CAN KNOW AND EXPERIENCE GOD'S LOVE AND PLAN FOR
YOUR LIFE.

He Died in Our Place
"God demonstrates His own love toward us, in that while we were yet sinners, Christ died for us"
(Romans 5:8).

He Rose From the Dead
"Christ died for our sins...He was buried...He was raised on the third day, according to the Scriptures...He
appeared to Peter, then to the twelve. After that He appeared to more than five hundred..." (1 Corinthians
15:3-6).

He Is the Only Way to God
"Jesus said to him, 'I am the way, and the truth, and the life; no one comes to the Father, but through
Me'" (John 14:6).

This diagram illustrates that God has bridged the gulf, which separates us from Him by sending His Son,
Jesus Christ, to die on the cross in our place to pay the penalty for our sins.

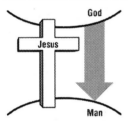

It is not enough just to know these three laws...

LAW 4. WE MUST INDIVIDUALLY RECEIVE JESUS CHRIST AS LORD AND SAVIOR;
THEN WE CAN KNOW AND EXPERIENCE GOD'S LOVE AND PLAN FOR OUR LIVES.

We Must Receive Christ
"As many as received Him, to them He gave the right to become children of God, even to those who
believe in His name" (John 1:12)

We Receive Christ Through Faith
"By grace you have been saved through faith; and that not of yourselves, it is the gift of God; not as a
result of works, that no one should boast" (Ephesians 2:8,9).

We Receive Christ by Personal Invitation

[Christ speaking] "Behold, I stand at the door and knock; if any one hears My voice and opens the door, I will come in to him" (Revelation 3:20).

Receiving Christ involves turning to God from self (repentance) and trusting Christ to come into our lives to forgive our sins and to make us what He wants us to be. Just to agree intellectually that Jesus Christ is the Son of God and that He died on the cross for our sins is not enough. Nor is it enough to have an emotional experience. We receive Jesus Christ by faith, as an act of the will.

These two circles represent two kinds of lives.

 S – Self is on the throne
† – Christ is outside the life
● – Interests are directed by self, often resulting in discord and frustration

 † – Christ is in the life and on the throne
S – Self is yielding to Christ
● – Interests are directed by Christ, resulting in harmony with God's plan

Which best describes your life? Which circle would you like to have represent your life?
The following explains how you can invite Jesus Christ into your life.

YOU CAN RECEIVE CHRIST RIGHT NOW BY FAITH THROUGH PRAYER
(prayer is talking to God). God knows your heart and is not so concerned with your words as He is with the attitude of your heart. The following is a suggested prayer:

> "Lord Jesus, I need You. Thank You for dying on the cross for my sins. I open the door of my life and receive You as my Lord and Savior. Thank You for forgiving my sins and giving me eternal life. Take control of the throne of my life. Make me the kind of person You want me to be."

Does this prayer express the desire of your heart? If it does, I invite you to pray this prayer right now, and Christ will come into your life, as He promised.

How to Know That Christ Is in Your Life
Did you receive Christ into your life by sincerely praying the suggested prayer?

According to His promise in Revelation 3:20, where is Christ right now in relation to you? Christ said that He would come into your life. Would He mislead you? On what authority do you know that God has answered your prayer? (The trustworthiness of God and His Word.)

The Bible Promises Eternal Life
"The witness is this, that God has given us eternal life, and this life is in His Son. He who has the Son has the life; he who does not have the Son of God does not have life. These things I have written to you who believe in the name of the Son of God, in order that you may know that you have eternal life"(1 John 5:11-13).

Thank God often that Christ is in your life and that He will never leave you (Hebrews 13:5). You can know on the basis of His promise that Christ lives in you and that you have eternal life from the very moment you invite Him in. He will not deceive you.

DO NOT DEPEND ON FEELINGS
The promise of God's Word, the Bible—not our feelings—is our authority. The Christian lives by faith (trust) in the trustworthiness of God Himself and His Word. This train diagram illustrates the relationship between fact (God and His Word), faith (our trust in God and His Word), and feeling (the result of our faith and obedience) (John 14:21).

The train will run with or without the caboose. However, it would be useless to attempt to pull the train by the caboose. In the same way, we, as Christians, do not depend on feelings or emotions, but we place our faith (trust) in the trustworthiness of God and the promise of His Word.

NOW THAT YOU HAVE ENTERED INTO A PERSONAL RELATIONSHIP WITH CHRIST
The moment that you received Christ by faith, as an act of the will, many things happened, including the following:

1. Christ came into your life (Revelation 3:20 and Colossians 1:27).
2. Your sins were forgiven (Colossians 1:14).
3. You became a child of God (John 1:12).
4. You received eternal life (John 5:24).
5. You began the great adventure for which God created you (John 10:10; 2 Corinthians 5:17 and 1 Thessalonians 5:18).

Can you think of anything more wonderful that could happen to you than entering into a personal relationship with Jesus Christ? Would you like to thank God in prayer right now for what He has done for you? By thanking God, you demonstrate your faith.

SUGGESTIONS FOR CHRISTIAN GROWTH
Spiritual growth results from trusting Jesus Christ. "The righteous man shall live by faith" (Galatians 3:11). A life of faith will enable you to trust God increasingly with every detail of your life and to practice the following:

    G Go to God in prayer daily (John 15:7).
    R Read God's Word daily (Acts 17:11). Begin with the Gospel of John.
    O Obey God moment by moment (John 14:21).
    W Witness for Christ by your life and words (Matthew 4:19; John 15:8).

T Trust God for every detail of your life (1 Peter 5:7).

H Holy Spirit—Allow Him to control and empower your daily life and witness (Galatians 5:16, 17; Acts 1:8).

FELLOWSHIP IN A GOOD CHURCH

God's Word instructs us not to forsake "the assembling of ourselves together" (Hebrews 10:25). If you do not belong to a church, do not wait to be invited. Take the initiative; call the pastor of a nearby church where Christ is honored and His Word is preached. Start this week and make plans to attend regularly.

Printed in the United States
By Bookmasters